Mu... ... ...

mmo
3414

TRADITIONAL
and
CONTEMPORARY

Oboe Solos

To the Oboists of the Future,

This project was created with the young oboist in mind and represents a great deal of artistic challenges I put forth as I look to the future of our instrument. I have dreamt of hearing the harmony behind some of our beloved solo works for years and I have finally found the means to achieve it by a combination of musical composition and the endless possibilities of electronic music.

Hearing harmony is an essential part of developing as a musician. As an oboist we are limited to playing single lines. I have expanded upon some of our most classical repertoire in hopes of advancing our playing abilities and our mind set as oboe players.

I would like to give special thanks to my teachers Allan Vogel, Melanie Wilsden and Robert Botti. Your support, encouragement and endless motivation continues to inspire me. This project is my contribution towards the advancement of the oboe.

Below I primarily discuss my thoughts on the various composers I have included in this project and overall musical feelings; rather than focus on my specific interpretation of their work. I feel the interpretation should and must be very much up to the individual player. The ultimate blessing of the oboe is that we are each able to develop a completely unique style of playing due to the amount of variables we work with; from the way we scrape our reeds, the way we blow, to the brand of the oboe we play and the embouchure we use. These numerous variables provide endless variations of tone and style that make each oboist unique. Personally the oboe has always been an outlet of artistic expression first and foremost. Expression is innately individual, unique and beautiful in every manifestation. The prime philosophy that I would like to impart on young oboists is to strive to develop a unique voice on the oboe with emotion emphasized above all else.

John Winstead 2015

TRADITIONAL *and* CONTEMPORARY
Oboe Solos

CONTENTS

ISBN 978-1-941566-90-9

Concerto in C minor
I.Introduzione

Domenico Cimarosa
Arranged by John Winstead

Larghetto

V.S.

Copyright © 2014

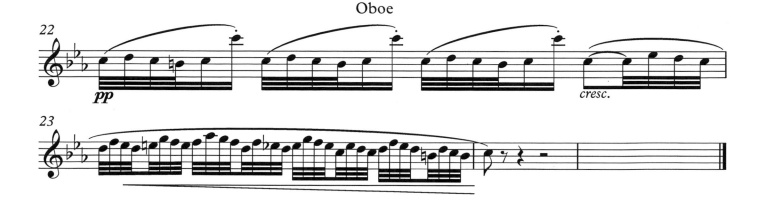

Cimarosa: Concerto in C minor (Introduzione)

Originally written as keyboard sonatas, Arthur Benjamin later took four of his favorite sonatas and combined them into the form of an oboe concerto. The theme from which the first movement of the oboe concerto is built on originally comes from the keyboard sonata 29. I have always been very fond of this introduction motif, it has a unique grace and elegance that feels timeless. I imagined and created the orchestration to sound somewhat aquatic, flowing and dream-like. The harp plays the right hand accompaniment while a thick organ bass plays the left hand. Finding the right style for this piece is a challenge. I believe the theme should sound elegant, flowing and never too urgent.

(page 4 of this music book)

Telemann: Fantasia III, Allegro

The Telemann Fantasies have become standard fare in the repertoire of the performing oboist. Played either in recital performance or as an encore work, they stand as a great test of both virtuosity and artistry. My orchestration of the allegro movement from the third fantasy fills out the harmony Telemann indicated and provides a background of thick strings to help support you as the soloist. I would advise you to practice the part alone with a metronome as the Allegro movement doesn't sway too far from dotted quarter = 120. Try to stay with the pulse of the orchestra and not get behind! The only concern for the performer are the empty measures at 14,15,16 (this motif is mirrored in the second section). In these measures the chord falls on beat one of each measure and immediately goes back into tempo at measure 17. My biggest piece of advice is to give this movement as much variety of tone, dynamics and colour as you can muster. Try to make each repeat different to keep the piece interesting and evolving, experiment with some choice ornamentation on repeats. The piece demands extreme flexibility of tone and great reed response.

(page 6 of this music book)

(dynamics left to your own discretion)

Fantasy III

G.P Telemann

Allegro

(2 clicks)

Oboe Concerto in F Major, RV.455

Antonio Vivaldi

0.0"
1.1
Vivaldi: Concerto in F. (RV455). 1st movement

Allegro Giusto

II. Grave

0.0"
1.1
Vivaldi: Concerto in F. (RV455), 2nd movement

Oboe

Bass

Vivaldi Oboe Concerto in F Major

I. Allegro Giusto: I left much of this concerto unedited. I wanted to leave many of the dynamics and articulations up to the player, while still giving you some framework. This first movement is musically simple but difficult technically. Try to create a vibrant and bright reed with enough aperture to capture the joyous mood of the piece. You can choose to play the tutti sections or use them as rests, this is up to you. My favorite thing about playing Baroque music is the amount of artistic influence you can have on the piece. Try to be as free as you can be within the beat. Variety of tone, dynamic and colour will bring the piece to life. Some choice ornamentation livens up the mood and adds variety (especially on repeats). *(page 7 of this music book)*

II. Grave: A beautiful and simple melodic interlude. Vivaldi did not score a full orchestration for this movement and instead wrote a solo violin part to accompany. In my accompaniment I used a solo synthetic voice playing the bass line that provides a sacred atmosphere. The tempo does not sway much from eighth note = 75. To make this movement sound right, think simple. Use as few ingredients (musically speaking) as possible to deliver a well defined and sublime offering. *(page 9 of this music book)*

III. Allegro: This final movement of the F Major concerto perfectly displays unbridled joy and sheer virtuosity. It is one of those rare pieces for the oboe that sounds terribly hard but is a breeze to play! The theme hinges around the triplet pattern and every imaginable major third interval in the key of F major and D minor. In preparation for this movement I suggest practicing your two octave F Major scale and working it up to a brisk tempo, as well as working on F Major and D minor in thirds. While practicing thirds notice how difficult it is to get a clean interval between your A and C. Each time you play the theme (beginning in bar 10) try not to cluster your sixteenth notes too close together. They must sound clean and elegant, remember they aren't 32nd notes. Try to provide the right amount of accents and legatos to the triplet measures on the strong beats (beat 1 and beat 3). Again I left most of the dynamics blank in this addition; I would prefer you as the performer to create a unique set of articulations and dynamics that work for you. *(page 11 of this music book)*

III. Allegro

V.S.

MMO 3414

The Six Metamorphoses after Ovid

for Solo Oboe & Ancient Voices

Composed by Benjamin Britten
Accompaniment and Arrangement by John Winstead

I. PAN

who played upon the reed pipe
which was Syrinx, his beloved.

(indicates lyre improvisation)

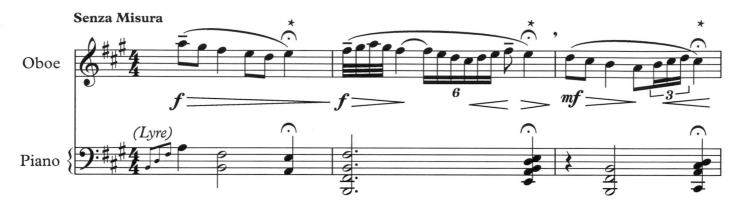

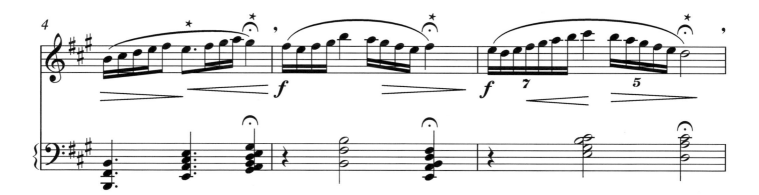

(indicates lyre improvisation)

MMO 3414

Lento ma subito accel.
(Begin with lyre pluck)

II. PHAETON

who rode upon the chariot of the sun for one day
and was hurled into the river Padus by a thunderbolt.

Vivace Ritmico
(begin at your leisure)

Britten: The Six Metamorphoses after Ovid

Benjamin Britten is regarded as one of the most prominent composers of the Twentieth Century. His music is a perfect mixture of widely accessible and avant-garde. At a young age he tapped into a style of composition that is unmistakably his own which can be heard with his second opus, Phantasy Quartet for oboe and strings. Britten had a lifelong love and fascination with Greek mythology and wrote numerous musical pieces venerating ancient tales. The Metamorphoses have become a stand alone monument in the repertoire of the oboe. The Six Metamorphoses serves as our finest solo work and a masterpiece in its own right. The piece revolves around a pantheon of minor Greek gods and goddesses. Each movement contains a musical adaptation of the God's journey and metamorphoses from Ovid's saga. My adaptation of this work has been the realization of a lifelong dream. I have performed the piece many times and it has always been my personal favorite work for the oboe. Many years ago I started to form ideas about sounds and harmonies I wanted to hear in the piece that simply don't exist; the crisp wind hitting the mountain top Pan plays from, the crash of thunder that brought down Phaeton's chariot, the hushed cries of strings underneath Niobe's tears after the death of her children and the fountain Arethusa becomes. There is so much content in each movement that I feel the oboe cannot fully represent the narrative by itself. I felt a work of such exquisite detail, breadth and magnitude deserved to be orchestrated and explored. I attempted to enhance the world Britten envisioned and provide a new perspective on the work.

(page 14 of this music book)

I. Pan: In Ovid, Pan pursued Syrinx the seductive wood nymph. She fled into the forest by the river Ladon attempting to flee him. Syrinx prayed to the gods to escape him and was granted transformation into a batch of reeds to avoid being caught. When Pan finally played on the handful of reeds that took her place; her soul could be heard in the sound of the reeds. I wanted to capture the sacred & ancient atmosphere Ovid describes as well as a hint of danger. My rendition includes howling winds on the mountain top, ethereal chords and a lyre that guides you through the movement. This arrangement is quite difficult to play with the accompanying track, I suggest listening to my recording for rubato & take note to follow the keyboard reduction as well as the solo oboe part; they both move as solo voices. With each * marked the lyre performs an improvisation that must be memorized in order to perform with the CD. If you wish to perform this movement live with keyboard you must create your own improvisations similar to the lyre on my recording.

(page 14 of this music book)

II. Phaeton: Phaeton was the son of Phoebus the sun god. Phaeton one day decided to fly his fathers chariot. Upon boarding the chariot the winged horses sensed that Phoebus was not operating the chariot and leapt into the sky. The chariot went straight up and immediately fell. A lightning bolt was thrown at the chariot to prevent the destruction of the earth upon impact Phaeton drowns in a river and we hear his air bubbles in the last measure of the movement. In contrast to the opening movement, Phaeton is a breeze to play with the atmospheric landscape I created. That being said, playing up to Britten's metronome marking is not easy! A crisp tempo creates the feel of the chariot flying through the sky; I suggest working the tempo up slowly. The overall articulation should be played quite short and harsh (as well as the articulation in Bacchus). Too often I have heard the Britten played like a Brahms sonata, I suggest a more literal interpretation of the work. Switch reeds between movements if you need to in order to achieve the proper sound and dynamics. A stable & ethereal reed is perfect for Pan, Niobe, Narcissus, Arethusa; while a reed with bigger aperture is perfect for Phaeton and Bacchus.

(page 16 of this music book)

III. NIOBE

who, lamenting the death of her fourteen
children, was turned into a mountain.

IV. BACCHUS

at whose feasts is heard the noise of gaggling womens'
tattling tongues and shouting out of boys.

III. Niobe: Niobe had fourteen children consisting of seven sons and seven daughters. She felt herself superior to the Titan Latona which offended the gods Apollo & Diana who then felt compelled to kill all of Niobe's offspring. Niobe was so sad from the death of her children she was transformed into a mountain. With my accompaniment I wanted to capture the magnitude of grief that Niobe embodies. Begin counting the four rests when you hear the strings and harp enter with flowing eighth notes. Notice the accent Britten indicated on the front of each dotted quarter note. This is not a sharp accent but rather a weight to the front end of the phrase. The marking piangendo literally means crying, try to convey the mood of absolute and total loss. Tempo begins to fluctuate at marking Chord 1, take your time with each phrase you play on top of the chord markings. At bar19 we are back in a steady tempo. The harp is playing running 32nd notes while the orchestra and choir moves on each quarter note; this section will take a few tries with the accompanying CD to match the tempo. Once you hit bar 19 the tempo stays constant until bar 24. Try to fit yourself into the chords as closely as you can with the running triplets here. The conclusion of this movement is straight forward but incredibly difficult to play in tune! Practice the Db major arpeggio with a tuner. One trick is to leave your Ab key down for the majority of this ending passage. As long as your bridge key is in adjustment i.e., screwed down enough (you can test this by holding an F# and hitting the Ab key with your left pinky). If you hear any change in tone when tapping Ab the screw must be turned clockwise more until there is no change in tone when you flick the Ab key. This is a useful trick with the Ab key whenever you want for more graceful slurs. Your air support is vital to being able to play the last few bars as written. The softer we must play, the more air support is required. Creating a tranquil atmosphere will require a combination of tremendous air support and a very good reed.

(page 18 of this music book)

IV. Bacchus: "Bacchus, at whose feasts is heard the noise of gaggling women's tattling tongues and shouting out of boys." Bacchus is the god of wine, ritual and fertility. In this movement I chose to omit any accompaniment and leave you to play on top of the sounds of a ongoing bacchanal. The sounds of children and women can be heard chattering, as well as a lyre strumming softly in the background. I suggest playing this movement with a certain amount of rawness and disregard for refinement. As an oboist I always strive for beauty of tone and refinement but that can easily ruin the atmosphere of this movement. You should give the impression of sounding drunk and stumbling! To sound stumbling I suggest fluctuating the swing of the dotted eighth notes, as well as varying the speed of your short little notes.

(page 19 of this music book)

*From this point the notes with upward stems
represent the reflected image of Narcissus,
and those downward stems Narcissus himself.*

V. Narcissus

who fell in love with his own
image and became a flower.

VI. ARETHUSA

who, flying from the love of Alpheus the
river god, was turned into a foundation.

V. Narcissus: The heart of Britten's Metamorphoses. Narcissus forms a quintessential Britten Aria. The fast little notes, the huge intervals and mammoth expressive depth; He gave us a lot to work with as interpreters. This movement is as difficult technically as it is artistically. You must take extreme care with the rhythm and the phrasing of this movement. Britten was extremely exacting with his music and when playing Britten I think it is important to play exactly what is written. He misses nothing in his musical dictation with dynamics and articulations. For this movement we play the character of Narcissus, starring into his own reflection. In bar 14 we begin playing two roles: one as Narcissus himself, a bold and expressive character, and the echo a more meek and tender phantom in the background. As the movement progresses the two characters gradually form into one and unite as Narcissus is turned into a flower (a variation of the death myth). The accompaniment I wrote is very straightforward, the tempo doesn't sway much from just under Britten's metronome mark of 84 (try practicing at 75 with the metronome). Your artistic impulses must fit within the beat, I suggest practicing this movement with a metronome before attempting to play with the CD. Make as much contrast as possible dynamically and with tone colors as you switch between Narcissus and the echo. At the Tranquillo the sound of night crickets stir in the air. This section is completely free of accompaniment, take your time and give your last note the utmost care. *(page 21 of this music book)*

VI. Arethusa: "Arethusa, who, flying from the love of Alpheus the river god, was turned into a fountain." Arethusa is a beautiful nymph who, similarly to Syrinx, was fleeing the advances of another god. She was swimming in a stream when she heard the voice of Alfeus, the lusty river God. She ran from Alfeus but she could not outrun him. Arethusa prays to Diana to protect her. Diana then creates a cloud to hide Arethusa but as Arethusa begins to sweat she is transformed into a stream. She flows into a crack in the earth and escapes. I intentionally created the orchestration for this movement to be grand and finalizing. This is the last movement and it should be played as such. I used a full choir to give a lush background to play on top of. The atmosphere must be sacred and flowing. The choir moves on each measure, this movement must be felt in one. The tempo stays fairly steady but you must be ready to react to entrances. If the timing gets slightly off keep going, there is plenty of pauses at the end of each line on the fermatas. At measure 42 we are lost in a thick forest, the bass chords are held starting where they are marked in the score (this is when you begin the phrase). At measure 62 you must start quite slow to match the chord timing; by measure 71 we are back in one. *(page 22 of this music book)*

Wesendonk Lieder

Suite for Oboe

I. Stehe Still

(Stand Still)

Richard Wagner
Arrangement by John Winstead

(Theme From Trisan & Isolde)

Wagner: Wesendonck Lieder (Suite for Oboe)

Richard Wagner is arguably the most controversial and influential composer of the 19th century and has always been a personal favorite of mine. His music is as revolutionary as it is transcendent. Wagner's vision for a new and colossal musical art form has transformed and elevated all music after him. His mark can be heard in nearly every composer after his death, from Mahler to Björk. Wagner sits in that special place, somewhere in-between the extremely small to the extremely vast depths of space and time. The suite I created was born from a song cycle Wagner wrote while working on Tristan und Isolde. The Wesendonck lieder and the Siegfried Idyll are his only two non-operatic works that are still performed regularly. I created the suite from three of the five Wesendonck songs which I have set for solo oboe and various accompaniment. Movement one (stand still) I scored as a duet between solo harp and solo oboe with a string section and clarinet which finishes out the movement. Movement two (In the Greenhouse) I scored for solo oboe and Indonesian gamelan orchestra. Movement three (dreams) I used for a full orchestra with piano. *(page 24 of this music book)*

I. Stehe Still (Stand Still): This movement needs to be felt in two. The opening motif is accented and rather harsh; really go towards the ends your phrases with your crescendos. At the mf dolce (bar 39) you must sweeten the sound immediately. The tempo drops slightly in this section and more so in the next theme which is directly from the opening of Tristan und Isolde. Think about maintaining this long phrase (bar 46) and making a drawn out crescendo to bar 53. At bar 54 the tempo remains constant; listen to the harp for eighth notes! At (A Tempo) the orchestra enters with a subsequent clarinet solo (which you can see in the que of the score). This last mammoth phrase requires delicate timing that you must memorize from therecording. Make as large of a crescendo as possible in true Wagnerian style. *(page 24 of this music book)*

II. Im Treibhaus (In the Greenhouse): I chose the Gamelan Orchestra for this movement for its mysterious and exotic qualities that match questioning and floating mood of the music. Wagner was a great pioneer of music and somehow this strange orchestration brings out the unusual nature of his music. Memorize your first entrance from the recording as it is rather hard to feel the beat. Overall the tempo of this movement stays fairly constant. Bars 30 through 34 are solo minus chords that are marked in the score. Take your time here and create a massive crescendo from bar 35 to bar 36. The ending of the movement takes great air support for low note response. Remember the softer and lower you play on the oboe the more air support is required. Another technique to help with low notes is pushing the reed more into your upper lip for a better low note embouchure. I like to use more upper lip for low notes, hardly any embouchure for middle register and for upper register more reed pushed into the lower lip. *(page 26 of this music book)*

III. Träume (Dreams): This movement is often played as a stand alone concert piece. The rhythm of this movement should be felt strictly in six. Listen to the piano for the flowing eighth note beat throughout the movement. I don't have much to say about playing this movement other than try to make long phrases; that is carry your air all the way to the end of a phrase rather than making an immediate decrescendo at the loudest spots. Try to pick a reed that has both response and a beautiful tone. It should sound effortless and floating like dreams. *(page 27 of this music book)*

Im Treibhaus

(In the Greenhouse)

Träume

(Dreams)

Richard Wagner

Music Minus One
50 Executive Boulevard · Elmsford, New York 10523-1325
914-592-1188 · e-mail: info@musicminusone.com
www.musicminusone.com

MMO 3414

ISBN 978-1-941566-90-9